Workbook

for

Who Moved My Cheese

An Amazing Way To Deal With
Change In Your Work
And In Your Life

An Implementation Guide to Dr.
Spencer Johnson's Book

Gelena Reads

This workbook is intended solely for educational and personal use. It is designed to complement and enhance the original book, **Who Moved My Cheese**, written **by Dr. Spencer Johnson.** The workbook provides exercises, activities, and additional content to aid in understanding and applying the concepts presented in the original book.

Please note that this workbook is not a substitute for the original book. It is recommended that readers use this workbook in conjunction with the original book to maximize their learning experience and comprehension of the subject matter.

TABLE OF CONTENT

How To Use This Workbook

Welcome to the interactive companion workbook for **"Who Moved My Cheese: An Amazing Way To Deal With Change In Your Work And In Your Life" by Dr. Spencer Johnson.** This workbook is designed to enhance your understanding of the book's concepts, provide essential key takeaways, and guide you through a personal assessment journey to help you navigate the changes in your work and life effectively.

Getting Started:
Begin your journey by reading the Summary of the Original Book. This section will provide you with a concise overview of the main ideas and insights from the original book, setting the stage for your exploration of its core principles.

Essential Key Takeaways:
Throughout this workbook, you will encounter dedicated sections for each chapter of "Who Moved My Cheese." In these sections, you will find Essential Key Takeaways that distill the most important lessons and concepts from each chapter. These takeaways will help you grasp the essence of the book's teachings, making it easier to apply them to your own life.

Personal Assessment Journal Prompts:

One of the workbook's central features is the inclusion of Personal Assessment Journal Prompts at the end of each chapter. These questions are intended to promote introspection and self-reflection. Take your time to answer these questions thoughtfully, as they will guide you in applying the book's principles to your unique circumstances.

Self-assessment Questions:
Towards the end of the workbook, you will find a comprehensive set of Self-assessment Questions that encompass the entire content of the original book and your responses to the journal prompts. These questions are intended to help you gauge your progress and growth as you work through the workbook.

Your Journey, Your Pace:
Remember that your journey through this workbook is personal, and there's no need to rush. Take the time to reflect on your answers, revisit the book's key takeaways, and adapt its wisdom to your changing circumstances.

Share Your Progress:
Feel free to share your insights, experiences, and progress with others. Whether it's a friend, a mentor, or an online community, discussing your journey can provide valuable support and perspective.

Embrace Change:

As you embark on this workbook journey, keep in mind the central message of "Who Moved My Cheese": change is inevitable, but how you respond to it can make all the difference in your work and life. Seize the chance for development and adaptation presented by change.

We hope you find this workbook engaging and transformative. It's time to discover how you can navigate the maze of change with confidence and success. Let's begin your journey of self-discovery and transformation today!

Summary

Chapter 1: A Gathering: Chicago
In this chapter, you find yourself in Chicago, where a group of individuals has gathered. They're discussing a common challenge - dealing with change. The city serves as a backdrop to introduce you to the theme of change.

Chapter 2: Who Moved My Cheese?: The Story
You're taken into a story where you meet four characters: Sniff, Scurry, Hem, and Haw. These characters represent different ways people react to change. Sniff and Scurry are quick to adapt, while Hem and Haw are resistant. The story sets the stage for understanding the core concepts of dealing with change.

Chapter 3: A Discussion: Later That Same Day
After the story, you join the group in Chicago again for a discussion. They reflect on the story of Sniff, Scurry, Hem, and Haw. Through this discussion, you start to grasp the importance of embracing change and adapting to new circumstances. The chapter dives deeper into the characters' reactions and their implications.

This book provides practical insights on handling change in both your work and personal life, using the allegorical tale of the cheese-moving mice and their human counterparts. It aims to help you navigate the challenges of change with a proactive and adaptable mindset, emphasizing the need to monitor change, adapt quickly, and let go of fear and resistance.

A Gathering: Chicago

Essential Key Takeaways

1. Change is Inevitable: The gathering of former classmates in Chicago highlights the fact that life has a way of changing unexpectedly. People often find themselves in situations they didn't anticipate. This chapter reminds us that change is a natural part of life, and it's essential to acknowledge and accept it.

2. Resistance to Change: Nathan's observation that people tend to resist change because they fear it is a common human reaction. Carlos, who was once fearless as a football team captain, admits to this fear. This chapter teaches us that even the most confident individuals can struggle with change. Recognizing and addressing this resistance is the first step towards effectively dealing with change.

3. The Power of Stories: Michael's revelation about a simple story that changed his perspective on change highlights the effectiveness of storytelling as a tool for learning and personal growth. Stories can simplify complex concepts and make them relatable. This chapter emphasizes the value of open-mindedness and willingness to learn from stories and experiences to adapt successfully to change.

Personal Assessment Journal Prompts

1. Reflect on a recent unexpected change in your life. How did you initially react to it, and why?

_____

_____

_____

_____

_____

_____

2. Identify a situation where you resisted change because of fear. What was the fear, and how did it affect your response to the change?

_____

_____

_____

_____

_____

3. Think about a story or experience that has influenced your perspective on change. What lessons did you learn from it, and how have they helped you navigate change in your life?

_____

_____

_____

_____

_____

_____

Who Moved My Cheese?: The Story

Essential Key Takeaways

1. Four Characters: This chapter introduces four main characters - Sniff, Scurry, Hem, and Haw. They symbolize different approaches to change. Sniff and Scurry represent those who are proactive and adapt quickly, while Hem and Haw symbolize those who resist change.

2. Finding Cheese: "Finding Cheese" highlights the importance of recognizing and adapting to changes in your environment. The characters find their cheese (resources or opportunities) in a particular location, which can change over time.

3. No Cheese!: This section emphasizes that change can lead to situations where there is no cheese. It underlines the need to accept the reality of change and not cling to old ways when they no longer yield results.

4. The Mice: Sniff & Scurry: Sniff and Scurry, being proactive mice, teach us the value of continuously monitoring our environment and taking prompt action when change occurs. They embody the concept of embracing change as an opportunity.

5. The Little People: Hem & Haw: Hem and Haw, in contrast, represent those who are resistant to change. They struggle with fear, denial, and the desire to maintain the status quo. Their experiences illustrate the consequences of not adapting.

6. Meanwhile, Back In the Maze: This section shows the ongoing journey of the characters and how they react when faced with change. It emphasizes that change is constant and ongoing, and one must remain adaptable.

7. Getting Beyond Fear: Overcoming fear is a crucial takeaway. Hem and Haw initially fear the unknown, but learning to manage and conquer this fear is essential for personal growth and success.

8. Enjoying The Adventure: Change can be seen as an adventure rather than a threat. Sniff and Scurry enjoy the process of searching for new cheese, teaching us the value of embracing change with a positive attitude.

9. Moving With The Cheese: The story encourages us to move with the cheese, which means adapting to change willingly and swiftly rather than resisting it. This is a key takeaway for effectively dealing with change.

10. The Handwriting On The Wall: Recognizing the early signs of change is crucial. The "Handwriting on the Wall" signifies the importance of staying aware and

responsive to subtle hints of change in your environment.

11. Tasting New Cheese: Trying new things and adapting to change can lead to new opportunities and personal growth. This section encourages us to be open to change and explore new paths.

12. Enjoying Change!: The chapter concludes by reinforcing the idea that change is a natural and positive part of life. It suggests that by embracing change, we can not only survive but thrive in a changing world.

Personal Assessment Journal Prompts

1. Four Characters: How do you react to change like Sniff, Scurry, Hem, or Haw? Which approach do you identify with the most?

_____

_____

_____

_____

_____

2. Finding Cheese: Reflect on a recent change in your life. What did you gain from the experience, and how did you adjust to it?

_____

_____

_____

_____

_____

_____

3. No Cheese!: Have you ever faced a situation where what you were relying on disappeared? How did you handle it?

_____

_____

_____

_____

_____

_____

4. The Mice: Sniff & Scurry: What proactive steps can you take in your life to monitor changes and adapt more quickly?

_____

_____

_____

_____

_____

_____

5. The Little People: Hem & Haw: Have you ever resisted change? What happened, and what might you have done differently?

_____

_____

_____

_____

_____

6. Meanwhile, Back In the Maze: How do you view change? Is it a one-time event, or do you recognize that it's an ongoing process?

_____

_____

_____

_____

_____

_____

7. Getting Beyond Fear: Think of a change that scares you. What steps can you take to overcome that fear and embrace the change?

_____

_____

_____

_____

_____

8. Enjoying The Adventure: How can you approach change with a more positive and adventurous attitude?

_____

_____

_____

_____

_____

_____

9. Moving With The Cheese: Are there any changes in your life that you're resisting? But what if you choose to embrace them?

_____

_____

_____

_____

_____

_____

10. The Handwriting On The Wall: Are there any subtle signs of change in your life that you've been ignoring? How can you become more aware of them?

_____

_____

_____

_____

_____

_____

11. Tasting New Cheese: What new experiences or opportunities could you explore by being more open to change?

_____

_____

_____

_____

_____

_____

12. Enjoying Change!: Reflect on a time when you embraced change and it led to personal growth or a

positive outcome. How will you ensure that happens again?

_____

_____

_____

_____

_____

13. How do you handle change when you notice it in your life?

_____

_____

_____

_____

_____

14. Are you quick to adapt and take action like Sniff and Scurry, or do you resist change like Hem and Haw?

_____

_____

_____

_____

_____

15. What's your approach when you face a situation with "No Cheese"?

_____

_____

_____

_____

_____

16. Do you actively monitor your surroundings and make swift decisions, or do you tend to procrastinate?

_____

_____

_____

_____

_____

17. Are there areas in your life where fear of the unknown holds you back?

_____

_____

_____

_____

_____

18. How can you overcome fear and embrace change more effectively in your life?

_____

_____

_____

_____

_____

19. Have you ever viewed change as an exciting adventure? How can you do this more often?

_____

_____

_____

_____

_____

20. Are you open to moving with the cheese, or do you tend to resist and hold on to the past?

_____

_____

_____

_____

_____

21. Do you pay attention to the "Handwriting on the Wall" in your life, recognizing early signs of change?

_____

_____

_____

_____

_____

22. Have you recently tasted "New Cheese" in any aspect of your life? Describe the experience.

_____

_____

_____

_____

_____

_____

23. How can you cultivate a mindset that enjoys change in your daily life?

_____

_____

_____

_____

_____

_____

24 Reflect on a recent situation where you resisted change. What could you have done differently?

_____

_____

_____

_____

_____

25. Are you currently facing a change that you've been hesitant to embrace? What's holding you back?

_____

_____

_____

_____

_____

26. What steps can you take to get beyond fear and uncertainty when faced with change?

_____

_____

_____

_____

_____

27. Describe a recent change that turned out to be a positive adventure. What did you learn from it?

_____

_____

_____

_____

_____

28. How can you encourage yourself to take more proactive steps when change is on the horizon?

_____

_____

_____

_____

_____

29. What strategies can you use to make the process of adapting to change smoother and less stressful?

_____

_____

_____

_____

_____

30. Are there areas in your life where you've been ignoring the "Handwriting on the Wall"? How can you be more attentive?

_____

_____

_____

_____

_____

_____

31. List three ways you can be more open to trying new things and embracing change in your life.

_____

_____

_____

_____

_____

_____

32. Reflect on a time when embracing change led to personal growth and new opportunities.

_____

_____

_____

_____

_____

_____

33. Think about a change you're currently facing. How can you find joy in the process of adapting?

_____

_____

_____

_____

_____

_____

34. What are the benefits of moving with the cheese instead of resisting it?

_____

_____

_____

_____

_____

_____

35. How do you typically react when change catches you by surprise? What can you do differently?

_____

_____

_____

_____

_____

_____

A Discussion: Later That Same Day

Essential Key Takeaways

1. Change Happens to Everyone: The chapter emphasizes that change is inevitable in both personal and professional life. It shows how various characters in the story represent different ways people react to change, from resisting it like Hem to embracing it like Haw.

2. Facing Fear of Change: It discusses how fear often accompanies change, but the power of imagining a better future, represented by Haw's journey, can help individuals overcome their fear and adapt to new circumstances.

3. Peer Pressure and Change: The chapter highlights the influence of peer pressure in organizations. It explains that when individuals collectively embrace change, it can create a positive environment that encourages adaptation rather than resistance.

4. Letting Go of Old Behavior: The idea of letting go of old behavior patterns is presented as a valuable strategy for dealing with change. Rather than focusing solely on changing external circumstances, the characters realize that changing their behavior and mindset is equally important.

5. Painting a Picture of New Cheese: The concept of visualizing a better future, or "New Cheese," is discussed as a powerful tool for motivating change. It helps individuals set a clear vision of what they want and provides the motivation to work towards it.

6. Sharing the Cheese Story: The chapter concludes with the idea that sharing the story of dealing with change can be a valuable tool in helping others navigate change. It suggests that organizations and individuals can benefit from spreading this knowledge to create a culture of adaptability.

Personal Assessment Journal Prompts

1. Reflect on a recent change in your life. How did you initially react to it? Were you more like Hem or Haw? Explain why.

_____

_____

_____

_____

_____

2. Think about your current peer group or colleagues. Do you feel supported in embracing change, or do you sense resistance to it? How does this influence your own attitude toward change?

_____

_____

_____

_____

_____

_____

3. Imagine a scenario where you need to make a significant change in your personal or professional life. Describe how visualizing the benefits of this change could help you overcome fear and hesitation.

_____

_____

_____

_____

_____

_____

Self-assessment Questions

1. What is the central theme of "Who Moved My Cheese?" based on the chapter titles?

_____

_____

_____

_____

_____

_____

2. In "A Gathering: Chicago," what initial impressions and reactions did the characters have about change?

_____

_____

_____

_____

_____

3. Describe the main characters introduced in "Who Moved My Cheese?: The Story."

_____

_____

_____

_____

_____

4. What was the catalyst for change in the story, as discussed in "A Discussion: Later That Same Day"?

_____

_____

_____

_____

5. How did the characters in the book initially respond to the changes in their environment?

_____

_____

_____

_____

_____

_____

6. What are the key lessons that can be derived from the experiences of the characters in "Who Moved My Cheese?"

_____

_____

_____

_____

_____

_____

7. How did the characters' attitudes toward change evolve throughout the story?

_____

_____

_____

_____

_____

_____

8. In what ways can the concepts presented in the book be applied to your work and life?

_____

_____

_____

_____

9. What strategies or approaches did the characters in the book employ to adapt to change effectively?

10. Reflect on a personal experience where you faced significant change and apply the principles discussed in the book to assess your response and adaptation.

Made in the USA
Coppell, TX
25 March 2024

30536630R00026